Learning about...

Date Due

ONTARIO

APR 10 '8		JUN - 9 1998
MAR 2 1992		
APR 13 1992	MAR - 4 1999	
FEB - 8 1996	JUN 03 1999	
JAN 28 1997	FEB 10 2000	
FEB 11 '97	NOV 16 2000	
MAR 24 1997	JUN 11 2002	
JUL 24 '97		
SEP 02 1997		
SEP 13 1997		
SEP 13 1997		
FEB 19 1998		
APR 18 '98		
MAY 9 '98		

DISCARD

Ontario is Canada's second largest province. It stretches from the Great Lakes in the south to the shores of Hudson Bay in the far north. More than one - third of the people of Canada live in Ontario, mostly in the southern part of the province. Large cities and **fertile** farmland are located along the shores of the Great Lakes. Huge forests of evergreen and **deciduous** trees stretch across **central** Ontario. Up in the far north, the bare rocks of the Canadian Shield surround Hudson Bay.

Guides dressed in 19th-century costumes recreate the days of the settlers for visitors to pioneer villages in Ontario.

Ontario's history goes back to the days of the **voyageurs** and the fur traders. Many of the old settlements and trading centers of the past have been rebuilt to show some of the province's history. In Thunder Bay you can visit Old Fort William, once a major trading post for fur traders. To find out how soldiers lived over 100 years ago, visit Fort George and Fort Erie near the Niagara River or Fort York in Toronto. At Upper Canada Village near Morrisburg or Doon Pioneer Village near Kitchener, guides in 19th-century costumes **spin, quilt, thresh, plough** and make candles and soap, just as the pioneers did over 100 years ago.

Canada's capital city, Ottawa, is in Ontario. In the early 19th century it was a small logging town called Bytown. It was named after the British Colonel John By of the Royal Engineers who built the Rideau Canal. The name was later changed to Ottawa and in 1857, Queen Victoria chose it to be the capital of the new colony, Canada. The Rideau Canal links the Ottawa River to Lake Ontario. In winter it becomes the longest skating rink in the world as thousands of people skate around on its frozen waters.

Changing of the military guard in front of the Parliament Buildings in Ottawa.

The government of Canada meets in the Parliament Buildings in Ottawa. The present buildings were constructed in 1916 after a fire destroyed all the **original** buildings except the library. From the centre of the main building rises the Peace Tower. It is nearly 100 metres tall. RCMP officers dressed in scarlet tunics guard the main doors on the Peace Tower. Each day in the summer, tourists watch the changing of the military guard on Parliament Hill.

The National Arts Centre in Ottawa, one of Canada's best known cultural centres.

There are many parks, monuments, theatres, museums, and art galleries in Ottawa. One of its best known buildings is the National Arts Centre where Canadian and foreign artists perform opera, theatre, ballet, and concerts. At the National Museum of Man displays show Canada's past history. Famous Canadian inventions are on show at the National Museum of Science and Technology. At the National Library and the National Gallery you can see special books and works of art.

The waterways of the Kawartha region are a favourite cruising ground for boaters, sailors, and canoeists.

Ontario hikers and campers can choose between huge wilderness parks such as Algonquin or Quetico and smaller conservation areas in Muskoka, Haliburton, the Bruce Peninsula, and along the Niagara River. Sailors and boaters choose the inland lakes and waterways of the Kawartha region, the channels of Georgian Bay Islands National Park, the 1000 Islands Park, or the Rideau and Trent-Severn Canal systems.

The Trent-Severn Canal in the Kawartha Lakes region follows the ancien war-canoe route of the Iroquois Indians and of the French explorer, Samuel de Champlain. The canal links Lake Ontario to Georgian Bay through a chain of 44 **locks** and a marine railway. The Peterborough and Kirkfield lift locks in this chain are the highest **hydraulic** lift locks in the world.

Part of the border between Canada and the United States runs through the Great Lakes. There are five Great Lakes: Ontario, Erie, Huron, Michigan, and Superior. Only Lake Michigan is entirely on United States **territory**. Together, the Great Lakes form the largest fresh water system in the world. Lake Superior is the world's largest fresh water lake in **surface area**. Manitoulin Island in Lake Huron is the largest island in any fresh water lake in the world.

The Horseshoe Falls on the Niagara River. These are the Canadian falls. There are water-falls on the American side of the river also. The boat in the picture is the Maid of the Mist. It takes tourists to the foot of the falls.

The Horseshoe Falls at Niagara Falls on the Niagara River attract thousands of tourists every year. The Falls are beautiful to see but they are also very useful. The force of the water rushing through hydro generating plants down-stream from the Falls turns huge **turbines** to make electric power. Queen Victoria Park at the Falls was the first provincial park in Canada.

The St. Lawrence Seaway was built to allow ocean-going ships to make their way up the St. Lawrence River to Lake Ontario. The ships travel through a series of channels and locks. The locks raise or lower the water level to allow ships to avoid **rapids** or to move from one part of the river to a lower or higher section. Because of the Seaway, ships from many nations now can make their way from the Atlantic Ocean to Canadian and American ports on the Great Lakes.

The Toronto skyline with the CN Tower, the tallest freestanding structure in the world.

Toronto, the capital city of Ontario, sits on the northern shore of Lake Ontario. Some **historians** think that the name "Toronto" comes from the Huron word "otoronto", meaning a "meeting place". Today, Toronto is a meeting place for people in government, business, sports, the arts, and for thousands of tourists from all over the world. More people now live in the metropolitan area of Toronto than in any other city in Canada. Metro Toronto includes the communities and cities of East York, Etobicoke, Scarborough, and North York, as well as the City of Toronto.

The Old City Hall (left) and the New City Hall (above),
behind the pool and fountains on Nathan Phillips Square.

Interesting landmarks in Toronto are the Ontario Parliament Buildings, the
University of Toronto campus buildings, the castle Casa Loma, the Royal Ontario Museum, the Ontario Art Gallery, the Ontario Science Centre, and Ontario Place. The favourite tourist **site** is the city's two-tower curving City Hall
and Nathan Phillips Square with its gardens, fountains, and reflecting pool.
Across from the New City Hall stands the Old City Hall, one of Toronto's
most beautiful buildings.

Toronto's newest and most modern concert hall: the Roy Thomson Hall.

Toronto has many great theatres. Artists and actors from all over the world perform in the O'Keefe Centre, Roy Thomson Hall, the Royal Alexandra Theatre, the St. Lawrence Centre of the Arts, Massey Hall, and the Young People's Theatre. Many young actors perform in the little theatres around the city. The Forum, an outdoor theatre-in-the-round at Ontario Place, can seat 3000 people. Plays, musicals, concerts, and **cabarets** can be enjoyed all year round in Toronto.

One of the many Ontario GO trains making its way to Union Station in downtown Toronto.

Toronto and the area around it are heavily populated. Over one million people work in the city. Large expressways, the subway system, and the GO trains help people travel quickly to and from the city. People who do not want to use their car in the city itself can take buses, streetcars, or the subway trains to get around. Toronto's subway system was the first in Canada and is still the largest in the country.

One of Canada's most famous theatres: the Festival Theatre in Stratford. It is the centre of the annual Ontario Shakespeare Festival, running from June to October.

Festivals of all kinds are part of summer in Ontario. Two of the province's festivals are world famous: the Stratford Festival in Stratford and the Shaw Festival in Niagara-on-the-Lake. The Stratford Festival became famous because of its excellent performances of plays by William Shakespeare, the great **playwright** from England. The Shaw Festival has plays by the British playwright George Bernard Shaw as its major attraction. Not only Canadian artists perform at these festivals but also many famous actors and actresses from Great Britain, Europe, the United States and other parts of the world.

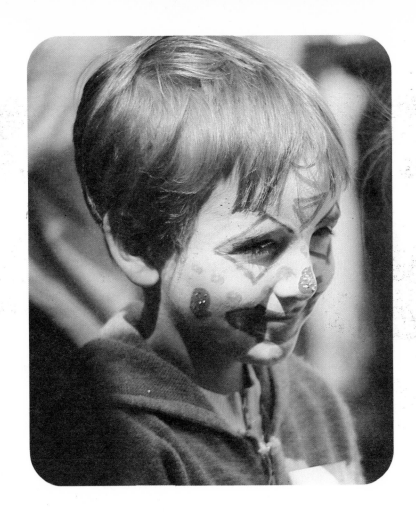

A "painted face" at the Canadian National Exhibition. Face painting is a favourite attraction for the young at the Fair.

Many small Ontario communities have fall fairs. At these fairs, farm families show their prize cattle, vegetables and flowers, home baking, and crafts. The Canadian National Exhibition, often just called the "CNE", is a larger kind of farm fair. It is the oldest and largest **annual** exhibition in the world. Its midway is Canada's largest. It has many exhibits and agricultural displays, sports events, a horse show, and an international airshow.

The home of Alexander Graham Bell in Brantford. Bell is one of Canada's best known inventors.

In the town of Brantford, Alexander Graham Bell, inventor of the telephone, made the first long-distance phone call. His home is now a museum. It remains furnished just as it was when Bell lived there and many of his inventions are on display. North of Toronto, at Kleinburg, is the McMichael Gallery. It has the largest collection of paintings by the Canadian artists known as the Group of Seven. It has carvings, paintings, and prints by Indian and Inuit artists.

"Chemical Valley" at Sarnia. It is Canada's largest oil-refining and petro-chemical centre.

In Oil Springs near the town of Petrolia, North America's first oil field was discovered. Near the site of the oil field you can visit the Oil Museum of Canada. It has working models of old-style and modern drill **rigs**. Ontario is not an oil-producing province but has an important oil refinery industry. Oil and gas from the west are refined at Sarnia, in an area called "Chemical Valley". The city of Sarnia is the most southern port for shipping Canadian oil and chemical products to the United States.

A car "assembly line" at a plant in Oshawa. In modern car assembly plants not all of the work is being done by people. Many parts of today's cars are being assembled by robots, machines that are guided by computers.

Oshawa and Windsor are the main centers of Canada's auto industry. There is also a large car assembly plant located near Oakville, west of Toronto. The car industry is very important to Canada because it provides work for thousands of people. Canada also imports many cars from many other countries, mainly from Japan.

To make cars, steel is needed. This steel is produced by **foundries** in the city of Hamilton. Hamilton is the center of Canada's steel industry. Because of its importance it is often called "Steel City" or "Steel Town".

At the town of Pickering, on the shore of Lake Ontario, is the Pickering Nuclear Power Station. Like the hydro generating stations on the Niagara River, the Pickering Power Station produces electricity. This electricity is made by the Canadian-built CANDU **nuclear reactor**.

A fishing and hunting lodge deep in the woodlands near Kenora.

Northern Ontario was once the hunting ground of Cree and Ojibway Indians. In the 19th century, fur traders hunted and trapped there. Today it is visited by thousands of men and women who canoe, hike, fish, and hunt in its **vast** woodlands. Many of the fishing and hunting lodges in northern Ontario can be reached only by small planes able to land on the many small lakes.

Open pit mining near the town of Timmins in northern Ontario.

Northern Ontario is rich in minerals. Mining is one of Ontario's major industries. Temagami, Sudbury, Blind River, Elliot Lake, Cobalt, Kirkland Lake, and Timmins are main mining areas. Ontario mines are producers of copper, nickel, uranium, cobalt, and gold, among many other minerals. These products are sent all over the world. Near the city of Sudbury visitors can go down into the Big Nickel mine to see miners busy at work underground. The INCO nickel mine is the largest producer of nickel in the world.

Logs cut to identical size are being shipped to pulp and paper mills around Ontario.

Northern Ontario has huge forest **resources**. These resources are used by the forest industry. **Softwood** trees such as black and white spruce are cut down for pulpwood. Pulpwood is used in the making of paper and paper products. **Hardwood** trees such as maple and oak are also cut and turned into boards, beams, planks, and other wood products for houses and furniture. When trees are cut down, small trees are planted to replace them so that the forest may grow again. This is called "reforestation".

Farmers market at Kitchener. Horsedrawn carriages mix with vans and trucks as farmers bring their produce to the market.

Agriculture is a major industry in Ontario. Seventy percent of all vegetables grown in Canada come from farms in southwestern Ontario. During the growing season, you can buy vegetables and fruits almost everywhere: at little roadside stands and old-fashioned farmers' markets, or you can pick your own in the fields. The Niagara Peninsula is best known for its fruits and wines, while the Holland Marsh and the Leamington areas are famous for all kinds of vegetables. Another crop, tobacco, is grown around the towns of Tillsonburg and Delhi.

Milking of cows by machines. It would take many people many hours to milk the many cows kept on the large dairy farms.

The Ontario landscape is **dotted** with dairy farms. Dairy farms raise herds of cattle for their milk. Ontario is a major producer of liquid milk. Many large farms are highly **modernized**. Milking of cows is done by machines. Milk from the farms is shipped to factories where it is put in bottles or cartons or turned into dairy products such as cheese, cream, and butter.

GLOSSARY

annual - happening once a year (p. 19)

cabarets - restaurants that offer shows with singing and dancing (p. 16)

central - at, in, or near the center (p. 4)

deciduous - trees that drop their leaves once a year, in autumn (p. 4)

dotted - to be located all over the place (p. 28)

fertile - able to produce good crops (p. 4)

foundries - places where metal is being made for use in objects such as cars or
bridges (p. 22)

hardwood - wood from trees that drop their leaves (p. 26)

historians - people who study and teach about history (p. 14)

hydraulic locks - closed-in sections of a river or a canal where water levels can
be changed by water pressure to raise or lower ships (p. 10)

modernized - to make modern (p. 28)

nuclear reactor - a machine that produces atomic energy to make power,
usually electric power (p. 23)

original - made first (p. 7)

playwright - writer of plays for theatre performances (p. 18)

plough - to turn and break up the soil before planting (p. 5)

quilt - to join together two layers of cloth with a soft pad in between, held in
place by lines of stitching (p. 5)

rapids - a part of a river where the water rushes rapidly, often over rocks (p. 13)

resources - natural resources are materials that are not made by people but are
produced by nature. Examples are coal, gold, water, lumber (p. 26)

rigs - equipment for building oil wells (p. 21)

site - place, location (p. 15)

softwood - wood from trees that bear cones, the evergreen trees (p. 26)

spin - to draw out wool or cotton on a spinning wheel and twist it into threads
that will be used to make clothes, blankets, table cloths (p. 5)

surface area - top area of a piece of land or water (p. 11)

territory - area of land (p. 11)

thresh - to separate the grain or seeds from wheat (p. 5)

turbines - engines driven by water, steam or air (p. 11)

vast - very large (p. 24)

voyageurs - name for the early French-Canadian explorers and fur traders. The
word means "travellers" (p. 5)

FACTS ABOUT ONTARIO

Surface Area: 1 068 582 square kilometres

Population: 8 854 700 (October 1983)

Capital City: Toronto

Major Cities: Ottawa, Kingston, Oshawa, Hamilton, London, Sarnia, Windsor, Sudbury, Sault Ste. Marie

Principal Rivers: Ottawa, Albany, Severn, Thames, Grand

Biggest Lakes: Superior, Huron, Erie, Ontario, Nipigon, Lake of the Woods

Provincial Flower: Trillium

Main Industries: Mining, Forestry, Agriculture, Dairy farming, Tourism, Manufacturing